WOMEN WHO ACHIEVED FOR GOD

12 Studies for Individuals or Groups

W I N N I E   C H R I S T E N S E N

Harold Shaw Publishers • Wheaton, Illinois

CONTENTS

INTRODUCTION

In industrialized nations the pressure to achieve runs high. This achievement is often measured by dollars, business or church expansion, and name recognition. People who are high achievers are admired or envied. They get things done; they get ahead. Unfortunately, in the scramble to the top, some are trampled under. Ambitious achievers can create enemies. They may personally suffer from stress. Tranquility does not seem to be one of the earmarks of success.

God undercuts our value system for success when he says, "It is the one who honors me that I will honor. . . People look on the outside; I look on the heart." Throughout Scripture we see the Lord continually putting his hand on people we might have ignored. He used them in significant, sometimes spectacular ways. Their accomplishments might not have made our local newspapers, but they are recorded for eternity in God's Word.

The women who achieved for God were from all walks of life. Some were slaves, some were poor, some were rich. They were mothers, singles, widows, aliens, women in royal households, women in business, women teachers, prophetesses, spiritual leaders, even rulers.

Women who were true achievers built on their personal faith in the Lord and used their abilities and opportunities with imagination and courage. As in every generation, there were those women who used their positions to personal advantage to exploit others. Those exceptions only serve to make the truly committed women shine brighter as those who "achieved for God."

In their accomplishments, women of God made an impact on their own generation as well as the generations to follow. They rescued nations, influenced kingdoms, advanced the cause of Christ, and didn't neglect individual friends or members of their families in their endeavors.

"Great is the company of those women who publish the Word of the Lord" (Psalm 68:11, a literal translation from the Hebrew).

HOW TO USE THIS STUDYGUIDE

Fisherman studyguides are based on the inductive approach to Bible study. Inductive study is discovery study; we discover what the Bible says as we ask questions about its content and search for answers. This is quite different from the process in which a teacher *tells* a group *about* the Bible and what it means and what to do about it. In inductive study God speaks directly to each of us through his Word.

A group functions best when a leader keeps the discussion on target, but this leader is neither the teacher nor the "answer person." A leader's responsibility is to *ask*—not *tell*. The answers come from the text itself as group members examine, discuss, and think together about the passage.

There are four kinds of questions in each study. The first is an *approach question*. Used before the Bible passage is read, this question breaks the ice and helps you focus on the topic of the Bible study. It begins to reveal where thoughts and feelings need to be transformed by Scripture.

Some of the earlier questions in each study are *observation questions* designed to help you find out basic facts—who, what, where, when, and how.

When you know what the Bible says you need to ask, *What does it mean?* These *interpretation questions* help you to discover the writer's basic message.

Application questions ask, *What does it mean to me?* They challenge you to live out the Scripture's life-transforming message.

Fisherman studyguides provide spaces between questions for jotting down responses and related questions you would like to raise in the group. Each group member should have a copy of the studyguide and may take a turn in leading the group.

A group should use any accurate, modern translation of the Bible such as the *New International Version,* the *New American Standard Bible,* the *Revised Standard Version,* the *New Jerusalem Bible,* or the *Good News Bible.* (Other translations or paraphrases of the Bible may be referred to when additional help is needed.) Bible commentaries should not be brought to a Bible study because they tend to dampen discussion and keep people from thinking for themselves.

SUGGESTIONS FOR GROUP LEADERS

1. Read and study the Bible passage thoroughly beforehand, grasping its themes and applying its teachings for yourself. Pray that the Holy Spirit will "guide you into truth" so that your leadership will guide others.

2. If the studyguide's questions ever seem ambiguous or unnatural to you, rephrase them, feeling free to add others that seem necessary to bring out the meaning of a verse.

3. Begin (and end) the study promptly. Start by asking someone to pray for God's help. Remember, the Holy Spirit is the teacher, not you!

4. Ask for volunteers to read the passages out loud.

5. As you ask the studyguide's questions in sequence, encourage everyone to participate in the discussion. If some are silent, ask, "What do you think, Heather?" or, "Dan, what can you add to that answer?" or suggest, "Let's have an answer from someone who hasn't spoken up yet."

6. If a question comes up that you can't answer, don't be afraid to admit that you're baffled! Assign the topic as a research project for someone to report on next week.

7. Keep the discussion moving and focused. Though tangents will inevitably be introduced, you can bring the discussion back to the topic at hand. Learn to pace the discussion so that you finish a study each session you meet.

8. Don't be afraid of silences: some questions take time to answer and some people need time to gather courage to speak. If silence persists, rephrase your question, but resist the temptation to answer it yourself.

9. If someone comes up with an answer that is clearly illogical or unbiblical, ask him or her for further clarification: "What verse suggests that to you?"

10. Discourage Bible-hopping and overuse of cross-references. Learn all you can from *this* passage, along with a few important references suggested in the studyguide.

11. Some questions are marked with a ♦. This indicates that further information is available in the Leader's Notes at the back of the guide.

12. For further information on getting a new Bible study group started and keeping it functioning effectively, read Gladys Hunt's *You Can Start a Bible Study Group* and *Pilgrims in Progress: Growing through Groups* by Jim and Carol Plueddemann.

SUGGESTIONS FOR GROUP MEMBERS

1. Learn and apply the following ground rules for effective Bible study. (If new members join the group later, review these guidelines with the whole group.)

2. Remember that your goal is to learn all that you can *from the Bible passage being studied.* Let it speak for itself without using Bible commentaries or other Bible passages. There is more than enough in each assigned passage to keep your group productively occupied for one session. Sticking to the passage saves the group from insecurity and confusion.

3. Avoid the temptation to bring up those fascinating tangents that don't really grow out of the passage you are discussing. If the topic is of common interest, you can bring it up later in informal conversation following the study. Meanwhile, help each other stick to the subject!

4. Encourage each other to participate. People remember best what they discover and verbalize for themselves. Some people are naturally shyer than others, or they may be afraid of making a mistake. If your discussion is free and friendly and you show real interest in what other group members think and feel, they will be more likely to speak up. Remember, the more people involved in a discussion, the richer it will be.

5. Guard yourself from answering too many questions or talking too much. Give others a chance to express themselves. If you are one who participates easily, discipline yourself by counting to ten before you open your mouth!

6. Make personal, honest applications and commit yourself to letting God's Word change you.

THE MIDWIVES AND JOCHEBED
Strong in Crisis

Exodus 1–2:10

Several generations after the time of Abraham, his descendants had multiplied into a nation: the Hebrew people. Faced with the threat of famine, Jacob and his family moved from Canaan to Egypt, where Jacob's son Joseph held a position of high responsibility in the Egyptian government. At the time of this opening chapter of Exodus, the Hebrew people are facing new problems.

1. What positive characteristics has your mother passed on to you?

Read Exodus 1.

2. In Genesis 46:3, God promised Jacob, "I will make you into a great nation there." From the story of Exodus 1, how is that promise being fulfilled?

3. After Joseph's death, why did the new Egyptian ruler consider the people of Israel to be a threat?

How would the Egyptian economy have been affected if the Hebrews had returned to their own land?

♦ **4.** What measures did the Egyptians take to counteract the Hebrew nation's phenomenal growth? How successful were they (verses 11-14)?

♦ *Indicates further information in Leader's Notes*

◆ **5.** When his first plan to limit the Hebrews failed, whose professional help did the king enlist, and for what purpose (verses 15-16)?

From verse 17, what characterized these helpers? How did this quality affect their decision?

◆ **6.** When the king asked why his second plan was also failing, how did the midwives explain?

7. What did the midwives actually achieve? How did God respond to their success (verses 20-21)? Why was their reward (verse 21) especially significant?

How did Pharaoh accelerate the infanticide (verse 22)?

Read Exodus 2:1-10.

♦ **8.** What would have been the differences between Pharaoh's daughter and the mother of Moses?

What consequences was Moses' mother accepting when she placed the child in the basket and put it on the Nile?

9. Miriam, Moses' sister, was probably around twelve years of age. What character and initiative did this young babysitter exhibit?

How may Jochebed have prepared her daughter to cope with the unexpected? What kind of atmosphere do you think pervaded the Hebrew community after the Pharaoh's orders were made known?

◆ **10.** Although a pagan, what kind of character did the princess demonstrate? What risks did she take?

What advantages could she provide for Moses?

11. Why would Jochebed's action in verse 10 take the same kind of faith and courage she had exhibited earlier?

How might she have prepared her son for this cross-cultural experience? Considering that all three of her children became leaders of the entire Hebrew nation, discuss what Jochebed really achieved from her slave home.

12. What principles from the lives of the midwives, Jochebed, Miriam, and the pharaoh's daughter can we apply to our own decisions and actions under pressure?

How can we influence our children to respond to crises and tensions with courage and stability rather than panic?

MIRIAM
Prophetess and Co-Leader

Exodus 2:23-25; 15:19-21; Acts 7:22-30;
Numbers 12:1-16

Miriam was considerably older than her brother Moses; her decisive action when he was still an infant had shaped his destiny. She had participated with God in the development of Israel's leader. As an adult, she also played an important role, but it was not without its pitfalls. Miriam's position in the nation's leadership was a complex one, and, more than anything else, her story lends insight into the process of *co*-leadership.

1. Have you ever been in the position to influence a leader? What did you do? What kind of temptations and opportunities are involved in such a position?

Read Exodus 2:23-25; 15:19-21, and Acts 7:22-30.

2. Review the incident that occurred when twelve-year-old Miriam was Moses' babysitter. What leadership qualities were already evident in her? How could she remain calm and display initiative, knowing her family was in danger for hiding her brother?

3. How might this childhood episode have prepared her for future responsibilities?

Think for a few moments, then share with the group any specific incidents from your childhood that prepared you for accepting challenging responsibilities as an adult.

♦ **4.** The verses in Acts summarize eighty years of history. How do you think Miriam felt after Moses' disastrous encounter with the Egyptian (Acts 7:24-28) at forty, when she, along with everyone else, had to suffer forty more years of slavery (Acts 7:30)?

According to Exodus 2:23-24, what was life in Egypt like for Miriam? What had been her calling during those years (Exodus 15:20)?

♦ **5.** As a spokesperson for the Lord, how may Miriam have encouraged the people during their slavery? Of what would she have reminded them?

6. Many years later, the Lord gave credit to Miriam, saying in Micah 6:4, "I sent Moses to lead you, also Aaron and Miriam." After their deliverance from Egypt what additional miracle did the Lord perform for the people (Exodus 15:19)? (The full account is given in Exodus 14.)

In this moment of triumph, how did Miriam exercise leadership?

Read Numbers 12:1-16.

♦ **7.** Miriam and Aaron used criticism of Moses' marriage as an excuse to express their real feelings about something else (verse 2). What was it?

Why would their question in verse 2 have some validity? What, then, was their basic problem?

In the past, how had God apparently communicated with Miriam and Aaron (verse 6)? What made this occasion different (verses 3-6)?

8. Who came to Moses' defense and what approach did he use (verses 7-8)?

Why do you think the Lord made such a dramatic issue of this incident?

9. How did Moses react to God's punishment of Miriam (verse 13)?

◆ **10.** How did Miriam's strong points as a leader also make her vulnerable?

How did Miriam's jealousy affect herself and all her fellow travelers?

♦ **11.** Why is power hunger among Christians destructive? Of what is it an indication? How can anyone, especially people in leadership roles, avoid the trap Miriam fell into?

12. From Moses' example, how should a leader handle criticism? What leadership qualities in both Miriam and Moses should we emulate?

DEBORAH
A True Leader

Judges 4–5

The book of Judges is set in the period of history between Joshua's conquest of Canaan and the time of Samuel, Israel's last judge before the monarchy was established.

A cyclical pattern characterized this era, summarized in Judges 2:6-19. When Israel rebelled against God with idol worship, God would allow surrounding pagan tribes to oppress them. When the people began to repent and cry to God for help, he would raise up a judge to deliver them from these enemies. Then they would prosper until they rebelled again, usually after the death of the judge, and the cycle would be repeated. With each cycle, Israel's behavior became worse.

1. Do you know of a situation where a woman stepped in to do "a man's job"? How was she viewed because of her action? What were the results?

Read Judges 4.

2. At this time how formidable was Israel's enemy (verse 3)? For how long had Israel been dominated?

What kind of morale would people have had by this time? How much confidence would they have in themselves as a nation?

♦ **3.** From verses 4-5, describe Deborah's various roles. What kind of credibility had she established among the people?

4. Judges 2:16-18 says that judges were "raised up" by God. This means that Deborah had received her appointment directly from God. What kind of confidence could she have?

Why would it be important for a judge to know she was appointed by God?

5. What executive order did Deborah issue to Barak? By whose authority?

Why was the military strategy significant? What guaranteed outcome did she declare (verse 7)?

6. What did Barak's initial response (verse 8) reveal about his attitude toward Deborah? How might his reluctance have affected the military conquest for the people as a whole (verse 7)?

What would Barak's reluctance mean to him personally (verse 9)?

7. After Barak marshalled his forces, what happened in the enemy camp? How might Barak have felt at that point?

Discuss Deborah's challenge and Barak's response in verse 14. Why do you think God waited for Barak to make the first move before becoming actively involved in the conflict?

◆ **8.** How effective was Barak's counter attack (verse 16)? Why did Sisera feel safe with Jael?

What did Jael accomplish and how did she do it?

♦ **9.** Why is it significant that Barak was pursuing Sisera? What do you think went through Barak's mind when he saw Sisera?

10. What human factors were essential that day for God to subdue the enemy? Why do we often hesitate to initiate action? To assume responsibility? What did all the people accomplish through cooperation (verse 24)?

11. How many of Deborah's predictions came true? How successful was her leadership?

Read Judges 5, The Song of Deborah.

This rousing song celebrates Israel's victory. It has been preserved not only as a record of historical events, but as a beautiful expression of praise to God. Deborah and Barak sang it as a duet.

12. What trait in people brings praise to the Lord (verses 2, 9)?

How did Deborah describe God (verses 4-5)? Herself (verse 7)? What added dimension does this title give to her character?

♦ **13.** For what were the people of Zebulun and Naphtali commended (verse 18)? In contrast to the people who refused to help (verses 16-17, 23), how was Jael's heroism honored?

14. What character qualities do you admire most in Deborah?

Though our culture and lifestyle are different today, in what specific ways should contemporary Christian women follow her example?

TWO WIDOWS
Participating with God

1 Kings 17:1-24; 2 Kings 4:1-7

In the period of history covered by the biblical writings, women were even more oppressed than now. There were not many protections for them. They were more or less property in many cultures, their security wrapped up in the men in their lives—husbands and sons.

Widows in particular were vulnerable during hard times—so much so that a number of Levitical laws (given by God to Moses) were designed to protect and provide for them.

Deuteronomy 10:18 says that God has special concern for orphans and widows. It is no coincidence that widows and their children were the recipients of miracles in the life of one of the most "miraculous" prophets, Elisha. By needing God's special assistance, these women also became special participants in God's plans.

1. Consider some widows you know. What are some of their unique needs—emotional, physical, and spiritual?

Read 1 Kings 17:1-16.

♦ **2.** What brought Elijah to Zarephath, a Gentile city? Until now, God himself had provided for Elijah; how did he now plan to provide for the prophet?

How do you think Elijah felt about this plan?

3. How did Elijah's first request test the widow's faith (verse 7)?

What message was she trying to communicate by her response to his second request (verse 12)?

4. What did the widow recognize about Elijah (verse 12)? What was revealed about her faith or openness to it by her response to his request?

5. What was Elijah's challenge to her? What specific encouragement did he give her? Why was this remarkable? How did she respond?

Read 1 Kings 17:17-24.

6. Describe the widow's next major test of faith. On what did she blame the death of her son? Why do you think she saw the situation in this way?

What did God do for her through Elijah?

◆ **7.** Look at the widow's last statement in verse 24. For the first time she is *sure* that the Lord's word is true. What does this say about her willingness to go along with the prophet up until now?

How did this widow become a partner with God? What did she achieve by keeping Elijah alive?

◆ **8.** How are you like this widow? In what specific ways can her example encourage you?

Read 2 Kings 4:1-7.

◆ **9.** Describe the extent of this woman's problem.

What was the attitude of her husband's creditor?

♦ **10.** What was Elisha's *first step* in helping the woman?

Why were his initial questions to her significant?

11. What characteristic did the woman display by her actions in verse 5? How *might* she have responded to Elisha's plan?

12. What did the widow's actions achieve for herself and her family? What part did the Lord play in her success?

13. Put yourself in this widowed mother's place. How do you think she felt as she knocked on her neighbors' doors? As she closed her own door and began pouring oil? As she kept on pouring? What thoughts do you think she had?

♦ **14.** What asset do *you* have that, if yielded to God, could be used to help others?

15. How can this widow's experience encourage you if you feel overwhelmed by your circumstances? Should you ask or expect God to use supernatural means to solve your problems? Explain your answer.

16. With these two women in mind, make a list of the resources you have. Make another list—of how your resources can be used for others. Now list some of your own questions and fears about the character of God and how God is or could be involved with your life.

THE SHUNAMMITE WOMAN
Sensitive to the Spiritual

2 Kings 4:8-37

Men have traditionally received more attention for their spirituality than have women—because men have had more positions of authority and were therefore more visible than women. However, it is often the women who are more spiritually discerning and more willing to spend time and energy on spiritual matters. In this story it is a woman who recognizes that she has been in the presence of a "holy man of God." She takes the initiative to welcome him and subsequently receives blessing beyond what she would have dared dream for herself.

1. What lengths have you gone to in order to be in the presence of someone you considered "holy"?

Read 2 Kings 4:8-17.

2. Why did the Shunammite first open her home to
Elisha?

Why did she want to go to the trouble of preparing a special room for the prophet?

Would her wealth automatically make her generous? Why
or why not?

3. What kind of perception did the woman display? How
was her husband involved in her hospitality?

4. How did she respond to Elisha's desire to reward her? (The NEB renders her reply, "I am content where I am among my own people.") What does this reveal about her character? Her motive for giving?

♦ **5.** What was lacking in her life? Why would she fear Elisha's promise to her?

What characteristics—both positive and negative—are - revealed by her statement, "Don't mislead your servant . . ."?

Read 2 Kings 4:18-37.

6. During this next crisis, how did the woman's actions and reactions compare to those of her husband?

7. What decisive actions did the woman take? How were these significant?

8. What do you think went through her mind as she rode out to find Elisha? What would she expect from him, and why?

♦ **9.** Why do you think she gave the answer she did to the questions asked her by Elisha's servant in verse 26?

What does her first statement to Elisha tell you about her?

10. How urgent was this matter to Elisha (verse 29)?

How did the woman respond to the situation, and how did Elisha respond to her?

♦ **11.** What was the Shunammite's response when her son came back to life?

12. What impresses you about this woman? What puzzles you about her? What about her response in times of crisis inspires you?

JEHOSHEBA
God's Undercover Agent

2 Kings 11:1–12:16; 2 Chronicles 22:10-12

Sometimes all it takes is one person to turn historical events in a completely different direction. One person who tried to change history was the wicked Athaliah (daughter of notorious Ahab and Jezebel), who united Israel and Judah through her marriage to Jehoram. He died after reigning eight years, and was followed by his son, Ahaziah. Ahaziah reigned one year and was killed. At this point, Athaliah tried to implement a plan that would drastically change the history of God's chosen people. But there was another woman in the palace who stepped in and prevented God's original plan from being thwarted.

1. Has there ever been a time when your "undercover" work significantly helped or hurt a situation? Explain.

Read 2 Kings 11:1–12:1 and 2 Chronicles 22:10-12.

♦ **2.** Following King Ahaziah's murder, how did his mother try to guarantee her power in the kingdom?

3. In light of Athaliah's purpose, why was Jehosheba's action so courageous?

Where did she hide her infant nephew? For how long? Why would this be a safe place?

4. As a descendant of the royal line herself, how else might Jehosheba have reacted to the situation? (Her father was Jehoram, but her mother was not Athaliah.)

5. During the years that they hid him, how do you think Jehosheba and her husband, priest Jehoiada, prepared Joash (Jehoash) for his role as king? What would they need to emphasize?

6. Describe how Jehoida, the priest, presented Joash to the people as king. How was the usurper, Athaliah, dealt with?

What effect did this change of leadership have on the nation (2 Kings 11:17-20; 12:2)?

◆ **7.** How do you think Jehosheba maintained her courage through all those years of hiding and waiting?

God had promised to David (Jehosheba's royal ancestor) that his "house" and "kingdom" would "endure forever" (2 Samuel 7:16). What did Jehosheba's act achieve?

8. How would Jehosheba have benefited personally through her act of faith?

Read 2 Kings 12:2-16.

9. What continuing influence did Jehosheba and her husband have on Joash?

What more could they have encouraged him to do (verse 3)?

10. As God's children, living in obedience to his Word, what risks may we be called on to take?

HULDAH
God's Voice in a Hostile Society

2 Kings 22–23:25; 2 Chronicles 34:1-8

Prophets have never had it easy in this fallen world. Jesus lamented in Matthew 23, "O Jerusalem, Jerusalem, you who kill the prophets and stone those sent to you . . ." One who spoke for God often had an unpleasant message to relate—and that to the ears of people who repeatedly rejected God and were hostile to any rebuke or correction. The nation had a long history of corrupting its prophets to the point that they no longer spoke what God said, but delivered "good messages" for bribe money.

The story of Huldah offers a startling picture. The kingdom of Judah is rampant with idolatry. A musty book is found in the rundown temple of God. Its message throws the country's monarch into a panic. He sends his advisers to—of all people—a *woman*, the wife of the temple's wardrobe man. Why Huldah? Because she was God's prophet. Would she risk telling God's truth?

1. Have you ever been hesitant to speak up on theological matters because you were a woman—or do you know of women who have reacted this way? Explain.

Read 2 Kings 22 and 2 Chronicles 34:1-8.

◆ 2. After such a long history of idolatry and rebellion toward God on the part of Judah's kings, who do you think so influenced Josiah that he made a drastic change of direction (2 Kings 22:1-2)?

3. According to 2 Chronicles 34:3, where did Josiah start his spiritual reform?

♦ **4.** What was Josiah's immediate reaction when the Book of the Law was read to him (2 Kings 22:11-13)?

Note: The Book of the Law was probably the Pentateuch, or at least a major portion of Deuteronomy.

To whom did the high priest and the king's representatives go to find God's message?

5. What were Huldah's credentials? By whose authority did she speak? How did she refer to the king in 2 Kings 22:15 and 18?

6. Why would it take courage for Huldah to transmit this strong warning to the king?

What message of personal consolation did she have for Josiah? On what basis did the Lord show such compassion?

Read 2 Kings 23:1-25.

7. What was Josiah's immediate response to Huldah's message? How many of the people did he involve? How did he remedy their ignorance?

8. What promise did Josiah make to God? Who joined him in this commitment?

9. In verses 4-20, note the people, pagan objects, and practices that had to be destroyed and forsaken.

◆ **10.** What was the purpose for keeping the Passover?

What made Josiah's Passover exceptional?

11. What made Josiah unique (verse 25)?

12. What part did Huldah's influence have in Josiah's life and thus the spiritual reform of the nation?

What could have prevented Huldah from speaking out?

13. What pressures threaten your willingness to speak God's truth in a hostile environment?

How have you dealt with those pressures? How can you plan to deal with them in the future?

ESTHER
Divine Destiny, Part 1

Esther 1–4

This Old Testament story of adventure, suspense, palace intrigue, power struggles, plots, and counter-plots matches any bestselling fictional thriller of today. Though the name of God is never mentioned, God's presence and sovereignty permeate every page.

The story is set in the capital of the Persian empire, Susa, during the period of history following the Jews' seventy-year captivity in Babylon. Jews were scattered all over the vast Persian empire, and Esther was one of these displaced persons, an orphan who had been adopted by her older cousin, Mordecai. To this day Jews keep the Feast of Purim in commemoration of Esther's heroic deeds. Esther means "star," and she shines starlike from the pages of the book that bears her name.

1. Have you ever been in a situation when this famous phrase would have been appropriate: "It's a dirty job, but somebody's gotta do it"? Explain.

Read Esther 1–2.

Because of the nature of this story, fairly lengthy excerpts of the narrative will be read in the group. It is recommended that group members also read the entire book of Esther for themselves during the course of this and the next study.

2. What words would you use to describe King Xerxes (Ahasuerus)? Why did he depose Queen Vashti?

What qualifications did he establish for choosing a new queen? What qualified Esther for conscription in the royal harem?

3. What was it about Esther that made such a favorable impression on the palace staff? What does this reveal about her?

4. Describe Esther's relationship with her adoptive father, Mordecai (2:7, 10-11, 20).

After a year of waiting, what did Esther request before being presented to the king (2:13, 15)? Why is this noteworthy? Why did the king select her?

5. What action did Esther take when she was told about the plot against the king's life?

To whom did she give the credit?

In what ways was God's provision already evident in her life?

6. As a God-fearing Jewish woman, what thoughts and emotions might she have experienced in her new setting?

How might you have reacted in similar circumstances not of your own choice?

Read Esther 3.

♦ **7.** How did the conflict between Haman and Mordecai develop? Why would Haman's demand be repugnant to Mordecai?

For the supposed insult received from one man, how appropriate was Haman's plan for revenge (verse 6)? How extensive (verse 13)?

8. List Haman's arguments to persuade the king these people should be annihilated. (He never mentioned them by name, and the king didn't ask for identification.)

In his ready agreement, what did the king reveal about his own character?

Read Esther 4.

9. How did Mordecai and the rest of the Jews express their distress over the king's decree?

How did Esther find out about the decree?

♦ **10.** What did Mordecai emphasize as the reasons behind the edict (verse 7)? How did Haman expect to be able to pay so much money into the treasury?

What did Mordecai want Esther to do (verse 8)?

♦ **11.** What lay behind Esther's fear of going to the king as Mordecai requested?

What did she risk if she refused? On what did Mordecai base his confidence for deliverance in verse 14?

12. What did Mordecai mean by his question in 14? With what critical issue did Esther have to deal to answer that question? In what way must each of us answer Mordecai's challenge?

13. Esther accepted the challenge with what specific stipulations?

Of what benefit is group support in a crisis? How do you think her quiet resolve affected those in the palace around her and all the Jews in Susa?

14. Have you ever been concerned enough about a problem to make a conscious decision not to eat, not to watch TV, not to sleep, etc., so that you could give yourself solely to prayer? If so, what were the results?

ESTHER
Divine Destiny, Part 2

Portions of Esther 5–10

Once in the position of being Xerxes' queen, Esther has to juggle a number of different interests. She must act appropriately as a queen—or risk the king's displeasure (he's already deposed one queen). She must look out for the welfare of her people, the Jews. And she must determine how best to deal with Haman, her uncle's crafty enemy—who also happens to be a close adviser to the king.

1. Recall a sensitive situation in which you had to act as a mediator or peacemaker. How did you handle it, and what happened?

Read Esther 5.

2. What was Esther's first answer to her prayer and fasting of Esther 4:16?

Describe Esther's strategy in presenting her problem to the king. Explain why her caution and timing were appropriate. What might have happened had she accused Haman immediately?

3. How could Esther have kept her emotions under such good control?

Evaluate her handling of this national crisis in light of 2 Timothy 1:7:

For God did not give us a spirit of timidity, but a spirit of power, of love, and of self-discipline.

Have you ever experienced the value of this kind of stability in a stressful time? Who is the source of the beneficial characteristics in this verse? How can we appropriate them for ourselves?

Read Esther 7.

◆ **4.** In pleading for her people, what fact was Esther forced to reveal about herself?

How would things have been different if she had hidden this fact?

How can we apply this same principle in a practical way to our identity as believers?

◆ **5.** What lay behind Haman's desire for personal revenge? Why is such an obsession self-destructive?

Read Esther 8:1-8, 10-12, 16-17; 9:5, 19, 26, 28, 32; 10:1-3.

6. Summarize what Esther accomplished for her whole race through courage, wise restraint, and passionate conviction.

How did her actions benefit Mordecai? How well was her own leadership established?

◆ **7.** In retrospect, what qualifications made Esther the right person to fulfill her unique assignment and change the whole picture?

List the choices she made throughout the story and their consequences.

8. From what you know of Esther from these studies, discuss how she combined the attributes of submission, self-sacrifice, servanthood, and obedience with strength, courage, initiative, and decisiveness.

How can this combination be a pattern for Christian women today?

9. What does Esther's story reveal about the sovereignty of God in individual lives? In nations?

10. Within the framework of God's sovereignty, how significant are the personal choices we make?

Read Mordecai's question of Esther in 4:14. Ask yourself the same question. For what purpose do you think God may have placed you in your particular "kingdom"?

MARY AND MARTHA
Friendship That Blesses

Luke 10:38-42; John 11:1-44; 12:1-11

Two important women in Jesus' life were Mary and Martha of
Bethany. They were both single, they lived in the same home, yet
they were very different personalities, each of them serving the Lord
in her own unique way. The friendship they shared with Jesus opened
them up to some special opportunities—and blessed Jesus, too, in
his ministry.

1. Discuss some aspects of close friendship—positive and
negative.

Read Luke 10:38-42.

♦ **2.** When Jesus and his disciples arrived at the village of Bethany, how did Martha welcome them?

On this particular day what was Martha's primary concern? How would you feel if thirteen guests suddenly arrived at your house for dinner?

3. What was Mary's primary concern? Describe the tension that developed between the sisters. Of what did Martha accuse Mary?

4. How did Jesus deal with this tension between these two sisters who were both friends of his?

In his gentle rebuke of Martha what did Jesus emphasize? What meant more to him than an elaborate meal? Why?

5. What positive characteristics did both Martha and Mary display?

In what ways did each woman try to show honor to their friend and teacher?

What can we learn about true hospitality from this incident?

Read John 11:1-16.

6. When Jesus decided to head back to Judea, why were the disciples fearful (verses 8, 16)? What did the disciples assume about Lazarus?

What ultimate goal did Jesus hope to realize through this event (verse 15)?

Read John 11:17-44.

7. Describe the scene in Bethany when Jesus arrived. Put verses 21-22 into your own words. What do you think Martha was really saying?

8. Of what was Martha certain concerning the future (verse 24)? What new information did Jesus give Martha about himself (verses 25-26)?

Today, if Jesus asked you the question in verse 26, how would you respond?

9. What did Martha communicate with her sister this time? Visualize the next scene in verses 29-35.

Martha and Mary raised the same question (verses 21, 32). How did Jesus' responses to them differ? Why?

How would you answer the same question openly asked in verse 37?

10. As close friends and followers of Jesus, what kind of
expectations might Mary and Martha have had? Do you
expect more or less of Jesus now than when you didn't
know him as well? What are the advantages and disad-
vantages of high expectations?

11. What two kinds of thinking are demonstrated in verses
39-40?

In Jesus' graveside prayer (verses 41-42) he showed a concern earlier voiced to his disciples (verse 15). What is it?
Why is this matter of belief so important?

Read John 12:1-11.

♦ **12.** In this visit of Jesus to the home of Simon the Leper,
how were each of his friends (Mary, Martha, and Lazarus)
expressing their friendship to him?

Who objected to the way Mary expressed her love, and why?

♦ **13.** Why would Jesus' words in verses 7-8 be of special significance to this family?

14. How were Jesus and his ministry benefited by the household of Mary, Martha, and Lazarus?

How did they benefit from his friendship?

What price did they pay for their relationship to Jesus (verse 10)?

How did their relationship to Jesus benefit the community (verse 11)?

◆ **15.** Think of your own relationship to Jesus. Has your trust grown as you have come to know him better? Could he trust you as a friend?

PRISCILLA
Disciple Maker

Acts 18:1-5, 18-20, 24-28; Romans 16:3-5;
1 Corinthians 16:3, 19; 2 Timothy 4:19

Some people who work the hardest receive the least recognition—precisely because they are too busy to maintain a high profile for themselves. There are relatively few verses that refer to Priscilla and her husband, Aquila. But those few verses indicate two lives spent for God's kingdom. Priscilla not only practiced hospitality, but traveled for the sake of discipling believers. Paul's mention of the believers that met in her house implies a home that was a hub of the Christian community in Ephesus, Rome, and Corinth.

1. Who do you know personally who has a real, positive impact on the spiritual growth of others? Describe the character and lifestyle of this person.

Read Acts 18:1-5, 18-20, 24-28.

◆ **2.** Where did Paul meet Priscilla and her husband, Aquila? Why had they been expelled from Rome? How did they support themselves?

While Paul lived and worked with them, what do you think they talked about (verses 4-5)? From Acts 18, describe what you know of their relationship with Paul.

3. When Paul left Priscilla and Aquila in Ephesus, what confidence did he apparently have in them?

◆ **4.** Describe Apollos. How did Priscilla and Aquila enhance this young preacher's ministry?

5. On what did Apollos base his preaching (verses 24, 28)? Why was he so receptive to additional teaching? Of what did Priscilla and Aquila obviously convince him? What does this reveal about their level of knowledge?

Read Romans 16:3-5; 1 Corinthians 16:3, 19; 2 Timothy 4:19.

After spending time in Ephesus, Priscilla and Aquila returned to Rome, but when Paul wrote his final letter to Timothy from his Roman prison, Priscilla and Aquila were back in Ephesus.

6. How does Paul describe Priscilla (Prisca) in Romans 16:3? For what were Paul and all the churches indebted to Priscilla and Aquila (Romans 16:4)? What added dimension did this news item reveal about Priscilla?

7. Besides receiving guests and conducting their business (Acts 18:3), for what other purpose did Priscilla and her husband use their home (Romans 16:5)? What atmosphere prevailed there (1 Corinthians 16:19)?

♦ **8.** From all the references, how would you describe Priscilla? Her attitude toward work? Toward moving? Her relationship with her husband? With Paul? With other people? With God? Why do you think Aquila could encourage his wife's spiritual insights and teaching ability without feeling threatened by them?

9. In what ways can Priscilla's example challenge a woman in this century? In what ways can you aspire to be a disciple maker?

IMPORTANT WOMEN OBSCURED BY HISTORY

Acts 9:36-42; 16:9-15; Romans 16:1-16; Philippians 4:2-3

Most of us can easily name the "majors" in the New Testament church—Peter, Paul, Timothy, Barnabas, etc. But do we *really* possess a complete list? Of course not. Most Christian workers throughout history have labored in obscurity. Even today, some of the "flashiest" church people are not necessarily the most deserving of the title *Christian*.

It takes some extra examination to find the numerous women who worked side by side with Paul and the other "well-knowns." Possibly we are slow to notice their names because our own culture has trained us to see women more in strictly family roles than in ministry roles. But these women were certainly known in the churches, and in several of his letters, Paul makes a special mention of their service.

1. Name several women who have made a substantial impact on your life. Briefly explain their influence.

Read Acts 9:36-42.

◆ **2.** What was distinctive about Dorcas (Tabitha)?

◆ **3.** What did the believers do after Dorcas's death? Why would they have sent for one of the leading apostles?

4. Describe the scene when Peter arrived in Joppa. What particular group had Dorcas apparently helped the most, and how?

5. What happened next, and what effect did it have on the community?

Read Acts 16:9-15.

6. Why did the apostle Paul and his companions go to Greece (Macedonia)? What was special about the Greek city of Philippi?

What activity did Paul and his party discover in progress in Philippi?

7. What do you learn here about Lydia and her background? Why was she a member of this prayer group?

How did she respond to Paul's message?

◆ **8.** Who else was reached because of her response to the message?

How would this event have encouraged Paul in his calling of verse 10?

How did Lydia participate in Paul's ministry?

Read Romans 16:1-16.

◆ **9.** Who was Phoebe, and what does Paul have to say about her?

♦ **10.** In verses 3-16, how many women are named among those whom Paul thanks and encourages?

What are some of the roles played by these women?

Read Philippians 4:2-3.

11. With what title does he refer to the two women, Euodia and Syntyche in verse 3?

♦ **12.** What kind of disagreement do you think the women were having, and why did Paul feel compelled to address them so directly in a letter to the church body?

13. In what ways do the examples of these "obscure" women encourage you in the work you do for God's kingdom?

> Therefore, since we are surrounded by such a great cloud of witnesses, let us throw off everything that hinders and the sin that so easily entangles, and let us run with perseverance the race marked out for us. ²Let us fix our eyes on Jesus, the author and perfecter of our faith, who for the joy set before him endured the cross, scorning its shame, and sat down at the right hand of the throne of God. ³Consider him who endured such opposition from sinful men, so that you will not grow weary and lose heart. (Hebrews 12:1-3)

LEADER'S NOTES

■ Study 1/The Midwives and Jochebed

Question 4. God had foretold the Hebrews' years of slavery when he made the covenant with Abraham in Genesis 15. Verse 13 of that chapter states, "Then the LORD said to him, 'Know for certain that your descendants will be strangers in a country not their own, and they will be enslaved and mistreated four hundred years.'"

Question 5. Sometimes God's people must disobey lesser authorities, as did Peter and the other apostles in Acts 5:17-29.

Question 6. The midwives' explanation may have been partially true since the Hebrew women would have been stronger, from their hard work, than their Egyptian counterparts. However, their actions were based on a deliberate decision (Exodus 1:17). The king probably spared the female babies because he thought Hebrew women would intermarry with the Egyptians; this would eventually eliminate the Hebrew race.

Question 8. Numbers 26:59 tells us that Moses' mother's name was Jochebed. She is also mentioned in Hebrews 11:23.

Question 10. In reference to the princess, the literal Hebrew meaning for the words "took pity" or "felt sorry" in Exodus 2:6 is "pity to spare." It was a compassion that moved her to positive action. Acts 7:22 states that Moses was "educated in all the wisdom of the Egyptians and was powerful in speech and action."

▪ Study 2/Miriam

Question 4. There is no record of Miriam being married.

Question 5. As a prophetess, she probably would have reminded the people of God's promise to their ancestor Abraham in Genesis 13:14-17.

As recorded in Exodus 3–12, Moses returned to Egypt after being in the desert for forty years. There God used him and Aaron to challenge Pharaoh to let the people of Israel go. When Pharaoh was reluctant to lose this vast resource of slave labor, God sent ten plagues as persuaders. The final plague was the death of all the first-born children in Egypt. That night the homes of the Israelite families were protected by the blood of freshly killed lambs painted on their doorposts (Exodus 12:13). The Israelites then went out of Egypt a free people. Miriam was in that great company, alongside her brothers, leading the people from bondage to freedom.

Question 7. Aaron had actually been appointed as Moses' prophet in Exodus 7:1; Miriam was also a prophetess, so they were not being delusional in claiming to have some authority of their own.

Question 10. It is generally believed that Numbers 20:1 refers to a time toward the end of the forty years of wilderness wandering. This would have placed Miriam well up in her 120s.

Question 11. Other Scriptures that lend light to this subject are Mark 9:33-35, Romans 12:3, and 1 Corinthians 3:3.

■ Study 3/Deborah

Question 3. Here are the orders given to judges in Deuteronomy 16:19-20: "Do not pervert justice or show partiality. Do not accept a bribe, for a bribe blinds the eyes of the wise and twists the words of the righteous. Follow justice and justice alone, so that you may live and possess the land the LORD your God is giving you."

Question 8. What is amazing about this incident is that Jael's husband's clan was friendly with Sisera's king (Judges 4:17). For her to have killed this military leader means that she must have thoughtfully considered what his death could mean to the nation of Israel. She was also willing to go against her husband and his clan. Her actions, though brutal, reveal a woman of foresight and courage.

Question 9. After his initial reluctance, it seems that Barak has developed the drive to chase Sisera personally and kill him himself. But when he comes into the tent and sees what Jael has done, Deborah's words probably come back to him: "the LORD will hand Sisera over to a woman" (Judges 4:9). On this day, a man is humbled by the example of two women who were brave enough to take action.

Question 13. "Most blessed of women" is an expression of highest honor in the Hebrew context.

■ Study 4/Two Widows

Question 2. During the reign of Ahab and Jezebel the spiritual condition of the nation had reached an all-time low. Idolatry, thanks to Jezebel and her Baal worship, was rampant. Elijah, the prophet of God, appeared before King Ahab to announce that it would not rain until he said so. Then he disappeared for the next three-and-a-half years. Ahab never stopped hunting for him.

Question 7. Elijah still had work to do, and whatever he did affected entire nations, because he was God's chosen prophet and miracle worker. Thus, the woman who aided him in any way was actually a partner to his many works.

Question 8. Not only did this woman show hospitality with her resources when she and her son had nothing to spare, but she used what faltering, doubtful faith she had. Her example should be encouraging to anyone who is still learning who God is and what it means to live by faith.

Question 9. What the creditor was setting out to do was completely out of line with the Hebrew system of ethics and justice. This woman and her children were being victimized. See Leviticus 25:39-43.

Question 10. When Elisha asked the woman how he could help and what she had in her house, he caused her to think *specifically* and to consider the resources she had on hand. In the midst of turmoil, most people become overwhelmed and fail to attack problems specifically; it is much easier to see the general picture of doom, but that only leads to despair and not to solution.

Question 14. God has often used whatever people "had in hand" to do great things. Moses carried a simple staff in his hand, and by it God performed numerous miracles, including the parting of the Red Sea. The boy David killed the giant Goliath with a slingshot and a few small stones. And Jesus used as an example of righteousness the widow who put her last few coins in the temple offering.

◼ Study 5/The Shunammite Woman

Question 5. Since she already recognized Elisha as a man of God, she could be criticized for doubting what he told her. On the other hand, she was a realistic woman, one not eager to accept any predictions that were out of line with the natural order of things. Considering all the false prophets and deceptive sales pitches that exist in the world, a woman—or anyone—must carefully scrutinize fantastic sayings.

Question 9. The Shunammite obviously wanted to "go directly to the top." It's possible that her initial answer to Gehazi was a way of putting him off so that she could talk with Elisha directly. Also, she was in grief—when she reached Elisha she couldn't even speak at first, she was so overcome. Probably she was saving all her strength to talk to the prophet himself.

Question 11. Years later the Shunammite woman was helped once again by Elisha. See 2 Kings 8:1-6.

◼ Study 6/Jehosheba

Question 2. In 2 Chronicles 22:2-4, we see that Athaliah's influence on her son while he was king was not commendable. She was undoubtably trained in evil by her mother Jezebel, a woman whose very name has become a synonym for wickedness.

Question 7. Although she was a woman, as wife of the priest Jehosheba would have had access to the religious writings of the nation. She and her husband Jehoiada may well have discussed the implications of Athaliah's murder raid on the house of Judah—and decided together what must be done. However, Jehosheba, as a member of the royal family, was really the only one in a position to kidnap the young prince.

■ Study 7/Huldah

Question 2. According to the laws of Deuteronomy, parents were to teach their children regularly the ways and laws of God. Evidently, Josiah—just a child when he took the throne—had a mother who adhered to these instructions in spite of the prevailing atmosphere in the kingdom.

Question 4. It is interesting to realize that though both Jeremiah and Zephaniah were prophets at this time, the high priest and the others didn't go to either of them for counsel.

Question 10. Passover observance was a reminder that God had freed the people from slavery—that they were God's people.

■ Study 8/Esther, Part 1

Question 7. Exodus 20:1-3 forbade a Jew to kneel before or worship anyone or anything other than God.

Question 10. Haman would be able to "pay" this money into the treasury from the goods that would be plundered from the murdered Jews. See Esther 3:13.

Question 11. See Deuteronomy 7:6-9; 1 Samuel 12:22, and Psalm 9:9-10.

■ Study 9/Esther, Part 2

Question 4. Moses lived by a similar principle. See Hebrews 11:24-25.

Question 5. For further study, consider the warnings of Psalm 9:16 and Hebrews 10:30-31. Apply them to Haman's situation and to injustices that you observe today.

Question 7. A statement made by Daniel, another Jewish expatriate in a pagan culture, may be appropriately applied to Esther: "the people who know their God will firmly resist" (Daniel 11:32).

■ Study 10/Mary and Martha

Question 2. In the Greek the word "also" is implied in Luke 10:39: "Mary, who (also) sat at the Lord's feet . . ." This may mean that Mary didn't just sit listening to Jesus but had fulfilled other responsibilities as well.

Question 12. According to Matthew 26:6 and Mark 14:3, this incident occurred in the home of Simon the Leper in Bethany.

Question 13. He is speaking to people who know recently and firsthand what it is like to have a loved one die. They had prepared Lazarus's body for burial. But they had also seen Lazarus live again. For Jesus then to refer to his own burial must have planted the idea in the minds of these three friends that he would also be resurrected. Considering their experience, they may have understood the resurrection of Jesus sooner than others in his circle of disciples.

Question 15. Read John 15:12-17 for Jesus' description of true friendship.

■ Study 11/Priscilla

Question 2. Priscilla and Aquila must have become Christians while in Rome.

Question 4. Here, as in most of the references to Priscilla and Aquila, Priscilla's name precedes her husband's. She apparently took the initiative in this spiritual instruction. Although she and her husband worked closely together as partners, she had the more prominent role.

Question 8. Tradition tells us that Priscilla ultimately died a martyr's death in Rome. Monuments were built to her, some of which still survive. One early church father referred to her as "the holy Prisca, who preached the gospel."

■ Study 12/Important Women Obscured by History

Question 2. When the leaders of the church in Jerusalem needed people to care for the needs of widows, they sought people with specific qualifications, listed in Acts 6:3. In order to minister in such a capacity, Dorcas would have exhibited spiritual maturity and leadership.

Question 3. Peter had just healed a paralytic in nearby Lydda. The people in Joppa heard that he was in Lydda—and had probably heard about the miraculous healing he had performed. They may have hoped that he could raise Dorcas from the dead.

It is also likely they would have called Peter with or without that expectation. Dorcas obviously played a pivotal role in the ministry of that church body, and her death would have had a substantial effect on the community. It would be quite natural for them to want the assistance of Peter at this time; much in the way churches today rely on "regional directors" during times of crisis or upheaval.

Question 8. Lydia "became Paul's first European convert and gave him hospitality, with Silas and Luke (Acts 16:14-15, 40). . . . Evidently a woman of rank (cf. Acts 17:4, 12) she was head of a household, and thus either widowed or unmarried. . . . She was a Jewish proselyte, engaging in prayers and ablutions at the riverside on the sabbath. . . . Lydia may be included in Paul's reference in Philippians 4:3, but since she is unmentioned by name she may have died or left the city. Her hospitality became traditional in the church there (cf. Philippians 1:5; 4:10)" *(The New Bible Dictionary,* p. 718. Wheaton, Ill.: Tyndale House Publishers, 1982).

Question 9. Phoebe, although referred to as "servant," could have actually been a deacon; the Greek word used in Romans 16:1 carries that meaning.

Question 10. In Romans 16:7, Junias may well have been a woman, although scholars cannot be sure, since a similar man's name existed. Significant in these verses is the mention of these women side by side with the men, indicating that Paul saw them all as co-laborers in the ministry of the gospel.

Question 12. "Apparently the dissension between these two women was so great that Paul feared it might have serious negative consequences on the ongoing work of the gospel. What that difference of opinion was we do not know, but there is no reason to assume that it was trivial . . . it may have been a very serious matter having to do with their work in the ministry . . . .

"It is important to note that in this matter of Euodia and Syntyche Paul does not suggest that the church 'elders' or 'authorities' take the matter in hand. Nor are these women told to be 'submissive' or 'silent.' They are admonished to handle the problem themselves" (Ruth A. Tucker, *Women in the Maze: Questions & Answers on Biblical Equality,* p. 98. Downers Grove, Ill.: InterVarsity Press, 1992).

WHAT SHOULD WE STUDY NEXT?

To help your group answer that question, we've listed the Fisherman Guides by category so you can choose your next study.

TOPICAL STUDIES

Becoming Women of Purpose, Barton

Building Your House on the Lord, Brestin

Discipleship, Reapsome

Doing Justice, Showing Mercy, Wright

Encouraging Others, Johnson

Examining the Claims of Jesus, Brestin

Friendship, Brestin

The Fruit of the Spirit, Briscoe

Great Doctrines of the Bible, Board

Great Passages of the Bible, Plueddemann

Great People of the Bible, Plueddemann

Great Prayers of the Bible, Plueddemann

Growing Through Life's Challenges, Reapsome

Guidance & God's Will, Stark

Higher Ground, Brestin

How Should a Christian Live? (1,2, & 3 John), Brestin

Marriage, Stevens

Moneywise, Larsen

One Body, One Spirit, Larsen

The Parables of Jesus, Hunt

Prayer, Jones

The Prophets, Wright

Proverbs & Parables, Brestin

Relationships, Hunt

Satisfying Work, Stevens & Schoberg

Senior Saints, Reapsome

Sermon on the Mount, Hunt

The Ten Commandments, Briscoe

When Servants Suffer, Rhodes

Who Is Jesus? Van Reken

Worship, Sibley

BIBLE BOOK STUDIES

Genesis, Fromer & Keyes

Job, Klug

Psalms, Klug

Proverbs: Wisdom That Works, Wright

Ecclesiastes, Brestin

Jonah, Habakkuk, & Malachi, Fromer & Keyes

Matthew, Sibley

Mark, Christensen

Luke, Keyes

John: Living Word, Kuniholm

Acts 1-12, Christensen

Paul (Acts 13-28), Christensen

Romans: The Christian Story, Reapsome

1 Corinthians, Hummel

Strengthened to Serve (2 Corinthians), Plueddemann

Galatians, Titus & Philemon, Kuniholm

Ephesians, Baylis

Philippians, Klug

Colossians, Shaw

Letters to the Thessalonians, Fromer & Keyes

Letters to Timothy, Fromer & Keyes

Hebrews, Hunt

James, Christensen

1 & 2 Peter, Jude, Brestin

How Should a Christian Live? (1, 2 & 3 John), Brestin

Revelation, Hunt

BIBLE CHARACTER STUDIES

Ruth & Daniel, Stokes

David: Man after God's Own Heart, Castleman

Job, Klug

King David: Trusting God for a Lifetime, Castleman

Elijah, Castleman

Men Like Us, Heidebrecht & Scheuermann

Peter, Castleman

Paul (Acts 13-28), Christensen

Great People of the Bible, Plueddemann

Women Like Us, Barton

Women Who Achieved for God, Christensen

Women Who Believed God, Christensen